Reiki For Beginners!

The Ultimate Guide to Supercharge Your Mind, Increase Your Energy & Feel Great By Unlocking The Power of Reiki

By Dominique Francon

© Copyright 2014

All rights reserved. No portion of this book may be reproduced -mechanically, electronically, or by any other means, including photocopying- without the permission of the publisher.

Disclaimer

The information provided in this book is designed to provide helpful information on the subjects discussed. The author's books are only meant to provide the reader with the basics knowledge of the topic in question, without any warranties regarding whether the reader will, or will not, be able to incorporate and apply all the information provided. Although the writer will make his best effort share her insights, the topic in question is a complex one, and each person needs a different timeframe to fully incorporate new information. Neither this book, nor any of the author's books constitute a promise that the reader will learn anything within a certain timeframe.

This book is for informational purposes only. You should always see your medical expert before starting any physical activity, or diet. By no means this book intends to replace the advice of a professional. Proceed at your own risk.

Table of Contents

Introduction

Chapter 1 – What Is All The Fuss About Reiki?

Chapter 2 – Traditional and Western Reiki – The Differences!

Chapter 3 – The Reiki Symbols And Their Meanings

Chapter 4 – The Three Pillars of Reiki

Chapter 5 – Reiki and the Aura

Chapter 6 – Learning the Basic Hand Positions and Their Healing Powers

Chapter 7 – Different Breathing Techniques to Heal & Get Energized

Chapter 8 – Using Crystals in Reiki Healing

Chapter 9 – Reiki Healing and Children

Chapter 10 – Reiki Healing and Yoga

Chapter 11 – Benefits of Reiki Healing (You Can't Miss This!)

Conclusion

Preview Of "Buddhism For Beginners - The Ultimate Guide To Unlock The Amazing Benefits of Zen Buddhism"

Dedicated to those who love going beyond their own frontiers.

Keep on pushing,

Dominique Francon

Introduction

I would like to thank you for taking the time to download this book; *'Reiki For Beginners: The Ultimate Guide to Supercharge Your Mind, Increase Your Energy & Feel Great By Unlocking The Power of Reiki'!*

This book is designed to give you the knowledge and understanding that is needed to supercharge your mind, increase your energy and feel great while using the different methods of Reiki healing. Can't Reiki alter your lifestyle and make you a better and healthier person? There are many methods which you can try and they are all bond to heal certain areas of your body and allow you to get rid of any negative energy you may be experiencing.

Many people feel that healing techniques in generally require you to take a lot of time out of your day to day life to feel the benefits however, Reiki healing is one of those healing techniques that requires as little or as much time as your wish to feel the effects and benefits, it is completely under your control!

Reiki healing doesn't need to just be an activity that you pursue on your own, make it a family adventure! Reiki healers have seen great results in children as well as adults; it can calm them down and make their concentration levels a lot higher. Make it a family activity and you will all feel healthier and better connected to one another as a happy family.

By using all the different methods of Reiki in this book, I am confident that you will enjoy and feel the great benefits in both a physical and spiritual way! Reiki healing can be used alongside many other healing practices such as yoga and healing crystals! They go hand in hand and increase the healing powers.

Are you ready for a BIG change in your life?

Let's get started!

Chapter 1
What Is All The Fuss About Reiki?

Reiki was developed in the 1880's by a Japanese Buddhist called Dr. Mikao Usui. Reiki means 'spiritually guided life force energy', it is a spiritual energy practice that helps reduce and ease stress and allows the person being healed and treated the energy of complete relaxation in a natural and safe manner.

By helping the body relax you allow the body to re-activate the body's natural healing energy. The techniques used tend to be hands on healing or palm healing and can treat the entire body from emotions, spirit, relaxation, security and wellbeing; this is also known as a method of oriental medicine and a form of self healing.

Dr. Mikao Usui started this healing tradition to ensure that people could be healed by professionals and also be healed by themselves. He would only teach and work with those who truly wished to be healed and would allow their souls to follow the Reiki principles.

The Reiki principles are seen as a valuable tool and technique when practicing Reiki; it allows the patients to become compassionate, generous and to be fully relaxed.

The Reiki Principles:

Just for today, I will not be angry.

Letting go of anger, brings peace into the mind. Anger blocks ones energy, it is an inner enemy.

Just for today, I will not worry.

Letting go of worry, brings healing into the body. Endless worry may hurt ones soul; therefore treatment is required throughout the entire body.

Just for today, I will be grateful.

Being thankful brings joy into the spirit. Simple things such as thanks, smiles and good words can make people happy.

Just for today, I will do my work honestly.

Working honestly brings abundance into the soul. Supporting your family will help you live a respectable life.

Just for today, I will be kind to every living thing.

Being kind brings love into the world. Appreciate your family, friends and elders.

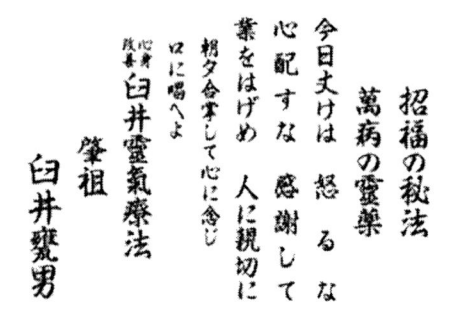

招福の秘法
萬病の靈藥
今日丈けは　怒　る　な
心配すな　感謝して
業をはげめ　人に親切に
朝夕合掌して心に念じ
口に唱へよ

心身改善　臼井靈氣療法

肇祖
臼井甕男

Dr. Usui passed away on 1930 and is know buried in Kyoto temple, the story of this life is written on this gravestone. It is believed that Dr Usui, taught and shared his Reiki techniques with eighteen masters before he died in 1930, one of these masters was called Dr. Chijiro Hayashi.

Dr. Hayashi became the second in line to Dr. Usui and opened a Reiki Clinic in Tokyo, his clinic both taught and healed patients and practioners. Dr Hayashi died on 10th May 1941.

Another master of Dr. Usui was Mrs. Hawayo Takata; she is recognized to have brought Reiki into the western world. She was taught by Dr. Hayashi, she was born in 1900, in Hawaii and treated many patients in the USA. It is believed that she trained up to 20 masters before she passed on 11th December 1980.

The Three Degrees of Reiki

There are three degrees of Reiki; ranging from healing and teaching one on one in the same room to distant teaching around the world.

The First Level

This is called proximity modality healing, the healers has to be near a patient physically to be able to heal them. This involves physical cleansing and can heal discomforts such as the common cold. This level of Reiki can be achieved in one day and is often used to improve the immune system and generally bust the health of those willing.

The Second Level

This is the next step up, it allows the healer to not only heal but teach Reiki across time and space. This means that the healing of Reiki can not only be sent around the world but it can also be sent into the future (time). According to healers in Reiki, time and space do not affect and limit the healing powers of Reiki.

This stage of Reiki is a lot more powerful then degree one, it is advised that the first level of Reiki is practiced for 3 months before level two is considered as it is a lot stronger and can bring back memories from the past and unresolved emotional issues that need to be healed.

The Third Level

This is split into three sections; the Master Healer, the Master (teacher) and the Grandmaster. If you are known as a Master healer you have achieved the highest level of Reiki healing. At this level of Reiki, the healing process can be sent just by thought so therefore the second stage of Reiki should be experienced for 1-3 years to allow the body to get used to the healing process. Positive thinking is essential for this level of practice.

A Master has the ability to teach Reiki to others but only levels one and two whereas the Grandmaster can teach Reiki at all levels.

Chapter 2
Traditional and Western Reiki – The Differences!

Traditional Reiki

Dr. Usui

Traditional Reiki is the method that Dr. Usui practiced by after a life a meditation, Buddhism and martial arts. The main goal of traditional Reiki is enlightenment and to be able to achieve a balanced life; he lived by the saying; *'If you can't heal yourself, how can you heal others'*.

The traditional Reiki methods focus on the principles and the use of meditation. The meditation is provided by breathing techniques which help direct the treatment directly to the area that needs healing.

Traditional Reiki is a way of challenging energy through your hands to restore health and well-being, the patient tends to be laid down on a treatment table and the practitioners hands stay still until they need to move the flow of energy through the body.

Western Reiki

Mrs. Hawayo Takata

This is the most common practice of Reiki and is focused mainly on the hands on healing component of Reiki. Not only is it focused on the hands on approach to healing it also includes the healing process known as 'Chakras'.

Chakras

Chakra is connected to the organs in our bodies and the different layer in aura. The word Chakra means 'wheel'; it is a wheel that spins on its own axis in relation to the energy levels in your body. The human body consists of many chakras bodily functions such as breathing, sensory, digestion, secretion, reproduction and circulation.

In total there are seven chakras points which can be focused on to help heal ourselves; the top the head, forehead (also known as the third eye), throat, heart, solar plexus, the navel and the bottom of the pelvis.

This picture shows the positions which can be focused on during Reiki healing through Chakras.

The top of the head (also known as the crown)

Identity, self knowledge and thought are all aspects of the crown element.

This does not just focus on the mind it is related to the whole body, the entire being. Once this chakras is developed it brings the patient wisdom, knowledge, understanding and bliss. It is the connection to the great world and our consciousness.

The third eye

Self reflection, light and identity are all aspects of the third eye element.

This belongs to the brain and facial features such as the eyes, nose and mouth. When this area is healed it allows us to 'see the bigger picture', to see clearly and get a better understanding of ourselves.

The throat

The aspects of this element are self reflection, creative identity and light.

This corresponds to the patient's throat and lungs; can be focused on when suffering with breathing problems. Once healed it allows us to have great creativity and communication.

The heart

This element has many aspects from social identity and self acceptance.

This chakra focuses on the heart and the arms. When this chakra is healed it allows us to feel compassion, love deeply and have a sense of peace and harmony.

The solar perplex

The aspects related to this element are self-definition and ego identity.

This covers many areas such as the liver, bladder, stomach, small intestine and the spleen. This is the power chakra, when it is healed and is healthy it brings us energy, personal power and a healthy metabolism.

The navel

Emotional identity and self gratification are both aspects of this element of the Chakras.

This chakra focuses on the reproduction systems, the urinary bladder and kidneys; it tends to be the focus when the patient is suffering from water infections or kidney pains. This is our connection chakras to other people through the feelings of desire and sensation. When healed this element brings us a great depth of feeling, sexual fulfilment and the ability to accept change in others.

The bottom of the pelvis (also known as the root)

The main aspects of this element are self preservation and physical identity.

This includes the large intestine and the rectum and can also help heal the kidneys if needed. As this chakras is located at the bottom of the spine it forms the foundation of our bodies, once healed this chakras should bring health, security and prosperity to the patient.

Chapter 3
The Reiki Symbols And Their Meanings

Traditional Reiki Symbols

In the Usui Reiki process there are five main symbols that are used to teach the processes of healing. The symbols alone do not hold any special powers in themselves; they are more used as a training tool when healers are training. All the symbols have their own intentions and this is what the healer or practitioner focuses on when using them, they energise the intention from the symbol.

The Power Reiki Symbol

The Japanese name for this symbol is *'Cho Ku Rei'* and the intention of this symbol is *Light Switch.*

Traditionally this symbol should be written left to right. The horizontal line represents the Reiki source, the vertical line is the energy flow and the spiral represents the seven chakras as it cuts the vertical line seven times.

The Japanese meaning is *'Place the power of the universe here'*. This symbol is used to increase the power of Reiki, but can also be used in reverse to decrease the power is needed. The light switch intention is used as a sign of protection and can instantly boost your ability to receive and channel Reiki.

This symbol can be used at anytime during the treatment but is most affective if used at the beginning, it will allow the person being treated to open up and receive more of the Reiki treatment, therefore allowing it to be more successful.

Uses of Cho Ku Rei:

- This symbol can be used to clear all negative energy from a room; this can either be done by drawing or visualising the symbol on the walls and the ceilings of the room.

- It can be used to protect you and loved ones.

- It can be used to increase the power of your healing abilities and can be used with other symbols to also increase their power. Visualise or draw the power symbol first.

The Harmony Reiki Symbol

The Japanese name for this symbol is *'Sei Hei Ki'* and its intention of this symbol is *purification.*

This symbol is meant to be visualised or written from left to right, the left symbol represents the left side of the brain (structure, logic and linear thinking) and the right symbol represents the right side of the brain (feeling, intuition and fantasy).

This symbol is used very similar to the Ying and Yang symbol by bringing balance to both sides of the situation. It is used to create harmony and peace, and is greatly used when difficulties are being faced. The Japanese meaning of this symbol is *'God and man become one'*. It is mainly used to release the negative problems and helps balance the left and right side of the brain. It can also be used to help improve mental issues such as nervousness, depression, anger and sadness.

Uses of Sei Hei Ki

- This symbol is a great tool that can be used to heal the misuse of different substances such as drugs, smoking and alcohol.

- It is a great tool to be used in the aid of weight loss.

- It is also a great way to improve your studying skills; it helps improve your memory and reading skills.

The Connection Reiki Symbol

The Japanese name for this symbol is *'Hon Sha Ze Sho Nen'* and its intention is to bring *timelessness.*

This symbol is to be written or visualised from top to bottom and represents the human body and the seven chakras. It is a very complex symbol and can come in many different variations.

The Japanese meaning of this symbol is *'No past, no present, no future'* this symbol has many purposes, from distant healing to spiritual connection. It is they symbol which is mainly used when sending Reiki treatments long distance and is therefore considered to be one of the most useful symbols in Reiki healing.

Uses of Sha Ze Sho Nen

- The main use of this symbol is to send Reiki healing to people in far distances away.

- Send Reiki healing into the future, helps support certain tasks that are needed to be fulfilled.

- It can also be used to send Reiki to the past, to release and heal trauma.

The Master Reiki Symbol

The Japanese name for this symbol is *'Dai Ko Myo'* and its main intention is to bring *enlightenment.*

The master symbol represents all that is Reiki.

This symbol signifies expanded wisdom and is used for the healing of the heart and soul. It can be used to heal diseases and illnesses as it centres our spiritual self.

Uses of Dai Ko Myo

There is only one use for this symbol and that is to be used as a reminder of the power of Reiki, its love and how it is available for everyone willing to open up and accept it.

The Completion Reiki Symbol

The Japanese name for the completion Reiki is *Raku* and its main intention is *grounding*.

This symbol is to be written or visualised from top to bottom, from the heavens to the earth. It represents a lightning bolt.

This symbol tends to be used at the end of a Reiki attunement process, the intention of the symbol is to ground the Reiki energy and helps achieve chakras alignment.

Uses of Raku

- To direct the healing to a particular part of the body that needs healing.

- Used to end the Reiki attunement process between a master and a student. Closes the teaching process.

Untraditional Reiki Symbols

There are some untraditional Reiki symbols which are not always used in Reiki healing. There are only some masters and healers that will use and teach these symbols and healing powers.

Zonar

This symbol can be used at the beginning of a healing session to prepare the body for deep healing.

This symbol is to be visualised of written in a certain way, firstly draw out the Z and then the infinity symbol, this should be written three times.

This symbol is used to heal past lives by healing the trauma that our memories hold. There are many different levels in which Zonar can work:

Cellular level – Zonar help release ad heal the memories and knowledge we have from the past.

Child abuse – it is used to help the trauma left behind from child abuse by healing our deep subconscious.

Harth

This symbol means love, balance, truth and harmony.

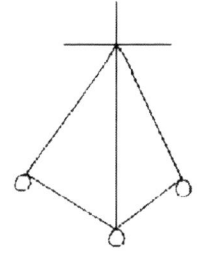

This symbol represents the heart, which love and healing flow through.

This symbol is mainly used to heal the heart and is used when there is healing needed within a relationship. It can also be a great way to deal with addictions from things such as drugs and alcohol.

Uses of Harth

- To heal relationships and heart problems
- Can help with addiction such as drugs and alcohol.

Rama

This Japanese symbols means *'abiding joy'* and its main intention is to help ground a person.

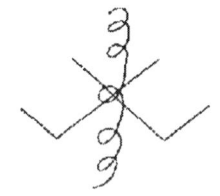

This symbol is to be written or visualised by firstly writing the straight lines then the spiral in the middle.

There are many areas in which Rama can be used to heal, from clearing the mind to harmonising the chakras.

Uses of Rama

- It is greatly used in the lower chakras; it is used to ground a person. It can help family identity and willpower.

- Can remove blockages from your feet and can release pain.

- Focus this symbol on the feet and it can be used to clear the mind, this feels great after a busy hectic day at work.

- Visualise Rama in the middle of a room; it can help clear out any negative energy from the room, which in turn can enhance your healing powers.

- It can help connect you with your higher consciousness and help you reach the goals in life you desire.

The Antahkarana

This symbol is known as the *'The master frequency symbol'* and its intention is to be *the bridge between two worlds.*

This symbol is a cube, with the number seven on each surface which represents the chakras.

It is known to help reduce and release the toxicity from your system and restore the happiness within you. You should focus this symbol in the room or below the healing bed and it will help enhance other symbols and healing powers, it connects greatly with the crown chakras, allowing positive thinking.

Uses of Antahkarana

- Create a positive mind set and help release negative feelings.

- Creates happiness and allows you to enhance other symbols to create greater powers.

Halu

Halu means beauty, truth and love and can also be used for harmony. The symbols intention is to *restore balance*.

This is an extension of the Zonar symbol, to write or visualise this symbol create the Zonar symbol and add the pyramid to the top.

This symbol is thought to be more powerful than the Zonar symbol and is used to restore balance. It is also used to get rid of negative thoughts and emotions from our bodies and minds. It can be used in many different ways to heal the body.

Uses of Halu

- It is a great help with achieving self acceptance and helps us take responsibility for our thoughts and actions.

- Use Halu with Zonar to increase the healing power, and it will help release traumatic emotions and feelings such as sexual or physical abuse.

- Helps us see to good in bad situations by bringing light into the dark areas of our lives.

- Helps by enhancing our personal power and strength; making us stronger emotionally.

Chapter 4
The Three Pillars of Reiki

As well as the five principle of Reiki there are also three pillars which Dr. Usui based Reiki around. This made it easier for people to understand, learn and teach to other people. The three pillars are called Gassho, Reiji-ho and Chiryo; they are different practices which are used within Dr. Usui healing system.

Gassho

The Japanese meaning for this word is *'two hands coming together'*, it is a meditative state where practitioners and healers centre themselves before giving and receiving treatments. This was practised at the beginning of all Dr. Usui's Reiki classes.

This is done by bringing your palms together in front of your chest while closing your eyes. All your attention should be focused on to the tip of your fingers, while clearing your mind.

Reiji-ho

The Japanese meaning of this word is *'indication of the Reiki power method'*, this method is used as a way of showing that we are willing to accept the Reiki power into our bodies.

This method is done in three parts:

1. The first step is to get into the Gassho position and allow the Reiki energy to flow through your body. The Reiki flow will either enter the body through the crown or the palms; these are both main access points of the chakras.

2. The next step is to ask for the energy to be passed through the client in question.

3. Then, hold your hands out in front of your third eye (forehead) and ask to be guided to where the healing is needed. You can either perform these steps out loud or in your head.

Chiryo

The Japanese meaning for this word is *treatment (medical)'*, this is done by the healer placing their hand on the patients crown chakras and waiting for the inspiration from Reiki for their hands to follow, also known as **hibiki** (*feedback*). This is a hands-on healing affect which can be great for physical painful areas of the body.

Chapter 5
Reiki and the Aura

The aura is known as the energy field around our bodies, it is electromagnetic and it interacts with the spirits through the seven chakras. The seven chakras are shown in our auras in different levels and can be shown through different energies. Our auras spread the entire way around our bodies, above our head and below our feet into the ground. Reiki healing can affect the aura in many different ways, the main affect is the strengthening of the aura, and it makes our aura spread from centimetres to meters. Reiki treatment not only helps the bodies organs and energy flow but it affects the entire aura that we have, great affects have been shown when the aura is treated from a distance.

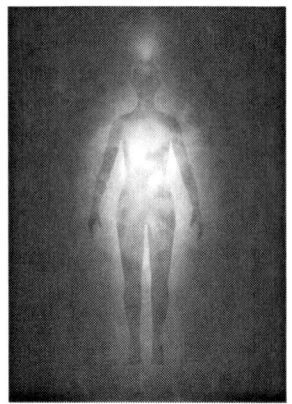

The different layers of Aura

The Physical body – this is the most tangible part of our consciousness, its main function is to help us achieve what we are doing at that particular time such as walking when walking, sleeping when sleeping and eating when eating. There are also three main fears that most people have of the physical body, these are sickness, aging and death.

The Etheric body – this is a very thin layer of the aura which surrounds the physical body, it acts as a template for the physical body. Our dreams tend to be captured in the etheric body as it is deeply connected to the root chakras. It helps us develop self acceptance and self love.

The Emotional body – the emotional body is egg shaped as it contains the physical body and the etheric body. The emotional body reflects the feelings and emotions our bodies have such as happiness, love, sorrow, hate, anger and hope. Reiki healing can help develop this layer to ensure that we can control our feelings otherwise they will become suppressed and can cause blockages within the navel chakras. The emotional body also helps us develop feeling and love for friends and family members.

The Mental body – the mental bodies function is to teach us self knowledge, logic, intellect and active thinking. This body is connected to the solar plexus chakras and helps with the bodies learning techniques and personality traits. If the person who is experiencing Reiki healing has a mental health or a mental illness in some way or another, this is shown in this layer of the aura and can therefore be easily healed.

The Astral body – this is the layer which consists of unconditional love and is connected to the heart chakras. This is the layer of the aura which is very emotional and can need the most healing at times. This is the layer that builds the bridge between the spiritual realm and the physical world.

The Divine will body (etheric template) - this is the layer of the aura which represents our memories and thought processes. All our memories whether they are forgotten or remembered are stored here. Not only are our memories stored here but the present and possible futures in our lives are also stored in this area of our aura. The divine will body is connected with the throat chakras.

The Celestial body – this is the mirror image of our subconscious mind and is connected to the third eye chakras. By listening to this layer of the aura your journey through life can be made a lot more simple and rewarding.

The Casual body – this is the last body of our auras and is where our creative impulses begin and is connected to the crown chakras. This is a very active layer of the aura and it is where our soul communicates with the conscious mind.

Different colors of the Aura and their meanings

It has been said that the more colourful and cleaner our aura is the better it is spiritually. In addition, the more consistent the energy spread is the healthier and more balanced a person tends to be. People tend to have one or two dominate colors in their auras, these tend to be their preferred or favourite colours. Now and again we will all flash other colors depends on what is going on in our lives.

Red Aura color meanings: these colors relate to the heart, circulation and our physical bodies. Red colors tend to indicate the following feelings; anger, forgiveness, nervousness, anxiety and obsessions. If the person is in a good, pure state then this color can provide a healthy ego.

Here is a clearer breakdown of the various shades which can be seen in the red aura and their meanings:

Deep red – active, strong willed, survival oriented, grounded and realistic

Muddied Red –anger

Clear bright red – passionate, powerful and energetic

Light Red – tender, loving, artistic, compassionate and sensitive

Dark pink – dishonest nature and immature behaviour

Red with orange tones – creative power and a high level of confidence

<u>Orange Aura color meanings</u>: orange toned colors relate to the reproductive organs and emotions. It is the color that shows good health, excitement, vitality, creativity, courageous natured and adventurous personality traits. It can also be the color that indicates stress related to addiction.

Orange with hints of yellow – this color shows personality traits such as; intelligence, perfectionism and detailed oriented.

<u>Yellow Aura color meanings:</u> this color relates to the life energy we have and to our spleens. A yellow color indicates easy-going, creativity, inspirational and playful traits. There are many different shades that can be seen in the yellow field, below is an explanation of each to make it clearer.

Pale yellow – positive excitement about a new idea they might be having, new ventures in life, hopelessness or spiritual awareness.

Bright lemon – fear of losing control in a relationship whether this is a personal or work relationship, respect and power.

Bright Gold – inspired personality and awakened spiritual energy and power.

Dark Gold, Brown yellow – overly analytical until feeling fatigue or stressed, making up for lost time through learning everything at once.

<u>Green Aura color meanings:</u> green relates to the lungs and heart, it is a healthy color of nature. An overall feeling of this color is the love of people, nature and animals.

Bright green – this color shows that the person is love-centred and is a healer.

Yellow/ Green – a great communicator and creative at heart.

Muddy forest green – insecurity, low self-esteem, blaming self, jealousy and resentment.

Greeny/ blue (turquoise) – this color relates to the immune system and can indicate a healer or a therapist.

Blue Aura color meanings: the color blue relates to the throat and thyroid. It is a cool and calm color and shows many personality traits such as; love, care, willing to help others and sensitivity.

Soft/ pale blue – light blue show peacefulness and clarity in a person's personality.
Royal blue – this shows a person high spiritual nature and that they are headed down the right path in life.
Dark blue – dark blue shows fear on many levels; such as fear of the future and fear of speaking or facing the truth.

Indigo Aura color meanings: this color relates to the third eye and shows deep feelings and sensitivity.

Violet Aura color meanings: the color violet relates to the crown and nervous system. Violet shows a sensitivity and wiseness about the person. They tend to be magical and artistic type people.

Lavender Aura color meanings: the color lavender shows a great imagination and day dreamer qualities.

Silver Aura color meanings: the color of abundance on both a physical level and a spiritual level. A flash of silver tends to mean plenty of money and wealth.
Bright silver – a nurturing personality who is very approachable to new ideas.
Dark grey – potential of health problems, especially if focused on one area of the body.

Gold Aura color meaning: gold represents protection and enlightenment; it shows that this person is being guided by a good spiritual force. Gold also shows protection and wisdom.

Black Aura color meaning: the color black pulls energy to it and captures the light. Black tends to indicate long term unforgiveness which can lead to health problems. Black can also show unreleased or hard to deal with grief that a person needs to release.

White Aura color meanings: this color shows purity within a person as well as truth angelic qualities. If there are flashes of white this can indicate that there are angels nearby and can also indicate that there is a soon to be pregnancy or that this person is already pregnant.

Earth Aura color meanings: earth colors represents colours associated with soil, wood and plants. This will show that the person is grounded and is seen in those that work outdoors or love to be one with nature.

Rainbow Aura color meanings: this is very important and is only shown in a few people. The color will beam from the persons hand, head and body and indicate that this person is a Reiki healer or is a star person; a star person is someone who is in the first incarnation on Earth.

Pastel Aura color meanings: if the colors in the aura tend to be a blend of pastel and light colors then this can show high sensitivity and need for serenity in this person.

Chapter 6
Learning the Basic Hand Positions and Their Healing Powers

Within Reiki there are many self treatment hand positions which can be learnt to start the treatments and to supercharge your bodies straight away. There are 12 main hand positions which are very effective.

All the following hand positions can be used to cleanse and heal your body and get rid of all the negative thoughts and feelings that you may be feeling.

Face position: Place the palms of your hands against your face, cup your hands over your eyes and place your fingers onto your forehead. Make sure that you touch your face lightly to allow the energy to flow.

The Crown position: Place both of your palms on the top of your head, with the heel of your hands resting near your ears. This will centre the energy through your body from top to bottom.

The Back of the head position: Cross your arms behind your head, place your right hand at the top of your head and your left hand just above the top of your neck; place your hands here lightly.

The Chin and Jaw line position: this is a great position for healing pain in the mouth. To achieve the healing from this position make sure that you rest your chin into your palms by cupping your hands then wrap your fingers around your jaw line.

The Neck, Collarbone and Heart hand position: Lightly grasp your neck with your right hand making a V shape around your chin. Place your left hand between your collarbone and heart, pressing lightly. This is a great position for heart problems and relationship healing.

The Rib position: This is a great position for any pain that is within the ribs. Lightly place your hands on the upper half of your ribcage making sure you have relaxed elbows.

The Abdomen position: Lightly place your hand on your stomach area (solar plexus area), just above the navel. Lightly touch your fingertips together. This is a great position for stomach pains and cramps.

The Pelvic bone position: Place your hands lightly over your pelvic bones and allow your finger tips to touch, this will allow the energy to run freely.

The Shoulder blade position: This is a great position for shoulder pain and neck pain; it can ease muscle aches greatly. Reach both of your arms over your shoulder, bend your elbows and place your hands lightly onto your shoulder blades. If you struggle to achieve this position, you can alternatively place your hands onto your shoulders.

The midback position: This is great for lower/ middle back pain and can help with muscle spasms and back tension. To achieve this position, place your hands behind your back and press lightly into the middle of your back.

The lower back position: This focuses the energy into the root of the chakras. The best way to achieve this position is to reach behind you and place your hands lightly onto your lower back.

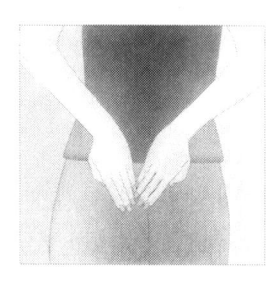

The Sacrum position: This hand position is another way to focus on the root of your chakras; it is a great way to relieve back pain. Reach behind you and place your hands just above your tail bone at the lower end of your back.

Leg position one: This hand position is great for any knee injuries and can reflect and ease any stiffness in your neck. To apply the energy place a hand above the knee cap and one under the knee cap, then focus on the pain.

The ankle position: wrap your hands around your ankles and focus all energy here. This will help treat any blockages that may be occurring within your lower body. It is a great method to help heal problems with the pelvic bone and thyroid gland.

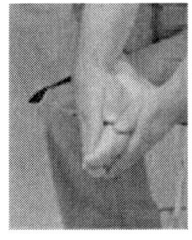

The foot position: place one hand on your sole; this should cover your sole. Place the other hand on top of your foot, wherever is comfortable. This is a great position for grounding your body and emotions. As your feet are the reflex zone for all of our organs, the entire chakras will be treated from this position.

Hands-on healing is a great way to introduce Reiki healing into your daily lives; it is a way to spiritually heal yourself and others around you that are willing to accept the Reiki healing. Practice these hand positions regularly and you will feel the positive energy healing your body.

Chapter 7
Different Breathing Techniques to Heal & Get Energized

One of the first steps of Reiki is to learn the basic breathing techniques as they help with the energy flow and healing processes. The main breathing techniques used in Reiki are deep breathing techniques which help both the healer and patient relax and absorb all the positive energy that can be released during a Reiki healing treatment. Not only with the deep breathing techniques allow the body to absorb the positive energy that surrounds it but it can assist you when connecting to the chakras.

There are many aspects to consider when practising the following breathing techniques. One way to focus the energy through your chakras is to imagine a light that is filling you as you breath in, focus moving the light to the area that needs healing, this will help you get through blocked feelings and energies which can be present in a body that is in need of Reiki healing.

The first breathing technique which needs to be practised and used when using the Reiki healing process is the *short breath*. This is generally how people breathe on a day to day basis however, you need to focus greatly on this technique, and clear concentration is needed. To achieve this breathing technique you need to breathe through your nose, filling your lungs fully before exhaling. When breathing in you need to concentrate on the universal energy and then when breathing out focus on pushing all the negative energy out of your body, releasing it from yourself.

The second breathing technique is inhaling while filling your lower body such as; diaphragm and stomach with air. While you are inhaling make sure that your stomach is expanding noticeably. Filling your stomach with air like this is a great way to meditate.

The third breathing technique that is used in Reiki healing is one where when breathing in you need to picture your ribcage filling with air and puffing out. To do this you need to take a long breathe in, to achieve this technique you need to first fill your lungs, followed by your diaphragm and then breath in deeper to expand your ribcage. This is a deep concentration breathing method and is a great way to relax while receiving and giving Reiki healing.

The Reiki breathing techniques are generally mostly effective when they are continuously practiced, like the saying goes 'practice makes perfect'. Learning the breathing techniques can be a great asset to your Reiki training and healing, it can place you in a more relaxed mood and can allow you to fully accept the Reiki treatment which you are receiving.

Chapter 8
Using Crystals in Reiki Healing

Crystals are not essential for Reiki healing but many people believe that they can enhance the experience of Reiki and the healing powers within. It is also another way to practise Reiki and can be enjoyable at the same time.

There are a few things that you will need to sort out before you can use crystals within your Reiki healing techniques. Firstly, you will need a different colour crystal for each area of the chakras; these can either be places on the area needing healing or near the area needing healing. There are many recommendations for the different crystals which can be used.

The crystals do not always need to be on or near the body, gather together the crystals which you wish to use and make a pattern out of them. Before using the crystals though they need to be cleanse of all negative energy, they can then be placed in a pattern and left somewhere in the room. The crystals are a great way to focus in healing sessions and can enhance the healing process in many people.

Here are some crystal suggestions to get you started:

Root Chakras:

The Red Tiger's eye

This will provide you with grounding, physical vitality and protection.

Garnet

The garnet will provide you with increased willpower, courage and survival instinct.

The Navel Chakras

Orange Calcite

This crystal will enhance your creativity and the positive energy surrounding your will and sexuality.

Carnelian

This crystal is great when healing is needed within a relationship.

Solar Plexus Chakras

Topaz

This healing crystal allows the body to experience confidence and self realisation.

Citrine

During Reiki healing this crystal will allow the patient personal power and the want to succeed.

Heart Chakras

There are four crystals which are great when Reiki healing is being performed on the heart Chakras:

Jade

Jade can be used when Reiki healing is needed for love, money, protection or healing of the heart.

Kunzite

This is a great crystal that can be used when Reiki healing is needed during love, luck and power.

Rose quartz

When a balance between heaven and earth needs to be achieved this is the best stone that can be used.

Aventurine

A great source of energy to help healing love and balance.

The Throat Chakras

Lapis

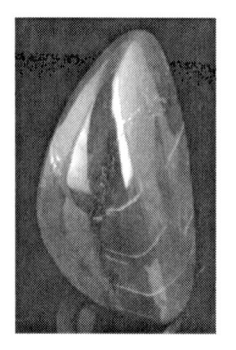

This crystal will allow you to have open communication.

Sodalite

When experiencing Reiki healing this crystal will allow you to speak openly and lovingly.

The Third Eye Chakras

Dark Amethyst

Using dark amethyst will help you get a clearer understanding of what needs healing.

Sugilite

This crystal is generally used to help teach patients love and forgiveness.

Crown Chakras

Light Amethyst

This crystal is used when focusing on the crown chakras as it enhances spiritual awareness and wisdom.

Clear quartz

The clear quartz allows the person receiving the Reiki healing to achieve a great spiritual connection.

Crystals are not traditionally used within the Reiki practises however, they are being used more and more and many people are finding that they help each other's powers and make the healing process more intense.

Chapter 9 – Reiki Healing and Children

Reiki is generally only associated with adults and many believe it should stay that way; however there are many healers which feel that Reiki healing is a great way to help children and babies

Reiki and Babies

Reiki has a calming effect so can therefore be great for babies, many healers have found that Reiki healing and massages have helped babies sleep better and has also improved their growth rates. There are many benefits which can be achieved from Reiki, when used on babies such as; reduced illnesses, improved colic symptoms, improved sleeping patterns, reduction of pain when teething and increased healing ability when injuries from falls are created.

Reiki and Toddlers

It has been proven that Reiki has great benefits when performed on toddlers and young children, the main benefit being an improved focus and memory within children and toddlers at school.

As toddlers will be relaxed during a Reiki treatment, this allows the healing process to work a lot quicker. By practising this process ten minutes a day it can decrease the hyperactivity and energy within your children.

Reiki and Children

By using Reiki healing in children it promotes a healthy way of living and will help them make better choices and will help create a great balance within their lives. There are many benefits which can help children who are being treated with Reiki healing such as; improved concentration, improved balance and calmness, reduction in signs of depression, enhances self esteem and confidence and improved symptoms of asthma.

Reiki and ADD or ADHD in Children

ADHD is the most common psychiatric condition which affects millions of children worldwide, some of the symptoms of ADHD are inattentiveness, hyperactivity, social issues, irritability and defiance. Reiki can help these symptoms with continuous treatment. A great way to get continuous treatment is by training in Reiki yourself, and then you will be able to treat your children on a daily basis.

Reiki and Autism in Children

Reiki can be a great healing practice that can be used for children suffering with autism. It can help calm children and allow them to focus on other things in their lives; it can improve their health and gradually get rid of fear, worry and lack of interest.

Getting Children Involved in Reiki

There are two activities which you can teach your children to get them involved in Reiki healing, the energy ball and the energy field. Have fun with these activities and your children will be interested in learning more about Reiki healing before your know it!

Energy Ball

This will teach your children to focus in on the energy around them. To do this make them place their hands together, get them to rub them together as if they were trying to warm their hands up. Get them to open their hands and place them with the palms facing each other and spaced about six inches apart, leave them there and just focus on the energy within their hands. What can they feel?

Gradually get them to move their hands closer together and then apart again and they should begin to feel the energy between their hands, it will feel like the energy is pushing their hands apart. With practice this energy ball will get stronger and stronger.

The Energy Field

This takes great concentration, get your child to stand completely still with their arms down and their palms facing the floor. Can they feel the energy around them? Get them to slowly walk towards someone else and see if they can feel the energy around them or in their palms.

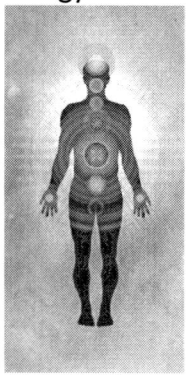

Chapter 10
Reiki Healing and Yoga

Many people feel that Reiki and yoga go hand in hand as the practice of yoga increases the flow and healing powers of Reiki in the human body. By practicing both healing techniques you will get a deeper understanding of both, they will enhance each other.

Yoga is a way in bringing a union together between mind, body and soul. A regular routine in yoga can bring great results in many therapies such as arthritis, asthma and heart problems. Not only can it help in these therapies it can also help those suffering with alcohol and drug addictions.

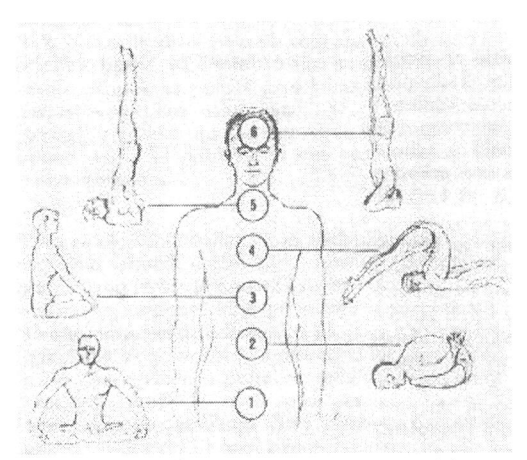

These are the main yoga positions which are associated with Reiki healing and the chakras.

There are so many different types of yoga, the main one which is used during Reiki healing is known as *Hatha yoga*, it is the combination of breathing and physical posture. The word Hatha literally translates as breath in and breath out, 'Ha' translates as 'in breath' and 'Tha' translates as 'out breath'.

Hatha yoga works by bringing the physical forces outside the body into alignment, through this alignment Reiki healing is increased through energy. There are 12 different positions which help the inner channels of energy open and allow Reiki healing to be absorbed.

The 12 postures:

While doing the following positions concentrate on the chakras area and allow the healing to begin.

- **Breath In and Out Chakras**: First Chakra **Body part**: Gonads

- **Breath In Chakras:** Second Chakra **Body part:** Pancreas and Circulatory System

- **Breath Out Chakras:** Third Chakra **Body part:** Adrenal Glands and Digestive System

- **Breath In**
  Chakras: Heart Chakra **Body part:** Thymus Gland and Respiratory System

- **Breath Out**
  Chakras: Throat Chakra **Body part:** Thyroid, Parathyroid Glands and Muscular System

- **Breathe In**
  Chakras: Third Eye Chakra **Body part:** Pituitary Gland and Skeletal System

- **Breathe Out**
  Chakras: Crown Chakra **Body part:** Pineal Gland, Brain and Nerve System

- **Breathe In and Out**
  Chakras: Root Chakra **Body part:** Circulatory System and Touch

- **Breathe In**
  Chakras: Second Chakra **Body part:** Digestive System and Taste

- **Breathe Out**
  Chakras: Heart Chakra **Body part:** Respiratory system and Smell

- **Breathe In**
  Chakras: Fourth Chakra **Body part:** Muscular System and Sight

- **Breathe Out**
  Chakras: Crown Chakra **Body part:** Skeletal System and Hearing

Each posture has a different intent to heal and achieve personal growth; they are used to open the body and to allow the flow of energy and Reiki to spread quickly between the different chakras. You do not have to practice these everyday to feel the effects, they can be practices as often as you like. Once these are practiced and learnt you will notice a change in your balance, stress and health – they should all improve!

Yoga Positions to Heal the Seven Chakras

There are many different yoga positions which can be used and practiced to maintain and heal a person through Reiki healing.

Chakra one:

This is the root chakras; there are three yoga positions which can be used to help heal any issue related to the root chakras. The following positions can help heal issues that you may be having with family, work, finances, trust and grounding. They can also be used to help physical issues such as; lower back pain, depression and problems in the immune system.

Position one: The Standing position

This is a great position to keep your body grounded; it will stabilize the base and root of your chakras. Here is how to do this position:

- Stand up straight with your feet apart, approximately 1-2 feet

- To release stress, pain, and drain unwanted energies from your body: focus on what you wish to release and heal, breathe in deeply bringing in positive energy and then breathe out fully, allowing all negative energy to leave your body.

- If you feel that your root chakras is incomplete: focus on drawing the positive energy from the ground and up through your body while breathing deeply in and out.

Position two: The Chair position

This position will allow you to stabilize your body and create great balance. Here is how to make the most from this position:

- Stand up straight with your legs slightly apart.

- Gently press your feet into the ground.

- Slowly start to bend your legs, allowing the gravity to take a little control.

- Raise your hands in front of you, find a comfortable bend position and hold for 10 seconds while breathing slowly.

Position three: The knee to chest position

This is a great position to help nurture your root chakras; here are the steps to follow to do the correct position:

- Lie completely flat on the floor, this will help ground your body.

- Slowly bring your knees up to your chest.

- Slowly breathe in and out and release all your negative energies.

Chakra two:

The second chakras is related to the sacral chakra, the following positions will be a great healing power if you are dealing with issues related to sexuality, identity, money, blame or guilt. They are also a great healing power when the person is dealing with medical conditions such as; back pain, urinary problems, bladder issues or problems in a person's genitals.

Position one: The Bow

This position has many different benefits such as; elasticity of your spine, healthy digestive system, healthy reproductive system and increases the energy flow of your body. Here are the steps to follow to get the best results from this position:

- Lie down flat on your front, your head facing down.

- While breathing in, bend your knees under you and reach back to hold your ankles.

- While breathing out, raise your head and chest and lift your knees and thighs from the floor.

- Look up and take a couple deep breaths, repeat this 5 times to feel the full benefits.

Position two: The Plough

There are many benefits to this yoga position, it can help with the flexibility in your spine and neck while strengthening your back, shoulder and arm muscles. There are a few steps that need following to make sure that all benefits are received:

- Lie down on the floor onto your back, legs together and your hands straight next to your sides.

- While inhaling bring your legs up, then exhale.

- While inhaling again, bring your hips up off the floor and support your back with your hands, keeping your elbows as close to you as possible.

- While exhaling, slowly bring your legs behind your head, do this without bending your knees. Hold this position for a few seconds and then slowly release your legs back to the floor.

Position three: The butterfly

This is the best position to practice to increase and encourage the energy flow within your sacral chakra. Here is how to practice this position:

- Sit with a straight spine and your feet together.

- Bend down and clasp your ankles with your hands, gently move your knees up and down, this will promote your body to relax and release negative energy.

Chakra three: The solar plexus chakra

There are many areas of the body which can be benefited from practicing yoga positions based on healing the solar plexus chakra. They can help with personal power, self respect, ego, individuality and self confidence. Not only can they help with these personal traits, they can also have great effects on your abdomen, kidneys, pancreas and medical conditions such as arthritis and diabetes.

Position one: Forward bend

This position has many health benefits such as fat reduction, flexibility of the spine and increased health in your nervous system.

- Lie flat on your back with your hands straight down besides you.

- While inhaling, come up to the sitting position with your toes pointing to the ceiling.

- Bend forward from the pelvic bone; stretch your arms above your head, straightening your spine.

- While exhaling, bend from your pelvis allowing your chin to come towards your shins while keeping a straight back.

Position two: The half spinal twist

The main benefits from this position are toning of the ligaments in your spine, flexibility in your spine and improved digestion.

- Kneel on the floor with your legs and knees together, sit to the right of our feet, lift your left leg over your right and place your foot against the outside of your right knee.

- Keep your spine as straight as possible.

- Inhaling slowly, stretch your arms out to the sides.

- Exhale slowly while twisting to the left

- While inhaling slowly, bring your right arm down and hold your left foot.

- Place your left hand down onto the floor behind you.

- Exhale slowing and twist as far as you can to the left and look over your left shoulder, hold this for a few seconds.

Position three: The cobra

This position is great for women and can help regulate their menstrual cycles and an pain during their periods. Here is how to do it:

- Lie down flat on your stomach, legs together and your palms down on the floor under your shoulders.

- While inhaling, raise your head and chest using your back muscles – hold this position for a few seconds.

- Exhale slowly and return back to the lying position.

- Inhale again, come back up as before however, use your hands this time and hold for as long as you can, take some slow deep breaths.

- Exhale and return to the lying position.

Chakras four: The heart chakra

This chakra is associated with love, compassion and forgiveness. The healing positions below can help a lot with issues such as; love, trust, compassion, grief, anger and loneliness. They can also help with physical problems such as asthma, lung and breast cancers, upper back pain and heart and circulatory systems.

Position one: The cobra

This is the same position from the chakras three; it will help on opening the chest and area around your heart.

Position two: The warrior

This position will help energise the shoulders and arms of your body while also opening the chest area. Here is how to make the most of this position:

- Kneel on the floor, sitting back onto your heels.

- While inhaling, stretch both arms out in front of you.

- Exhale slowly, raise your left arm over your head, bend at the elbow and allow your left hand to sit at the top of your back. Inhaling slowly.

- Exhale slowly while reaching your right arm round your right side, bend at the elbow and reach up your back.

- Make sure you have a straight back; if your hand can touch then link them together. Hold this position and breathe in and out slowly.

Position three: The Bridge

This position will help strengthen your back muscles and abdominal muscles. It is pretty easy to do and practice:

- Lie down on to your back, bend your knees up and place your feet flat on the floor, close together.

- Place your hands on the lower part of your back and lift your hips up as high as you can.

- Hold this pose for five seconds if you can, then lie down and relax.

Chakra five: Throat chakra

These positions help heal areas in the throat chakras; self expression and self will. Many issues can be healed here from following your dreams to using your personal power. There are many physical areas which can also be healed; the throat, teeth, gums, voice and neck.

Position one: The shoulder stand

This position will help rejuvenate the whole body, the entire chakras!

- Lie down on your back, palms down and by your sides and legs together.
- Inhale slowly, push your hands into the ground and raise your legs straight up above you, lifting your hips off the floor.

- Exhaling; bend your arms and support your back while pushing your legs up and high as you can.
- Straighten your back and bring your legs up straight, breathe in and out slowly.

Position two: The camel pose

This position helps greatly with blood flow and allowing energy to flow quickly round your body.

- Sit onto your heels and hold your hands behind you, one in the other.
- Breathing slowly in and out, let your head drop backwards and bring your hands up as far as possible.
- Hold this as long as possible, and then repeat as often as possible.

Position three: The fish

This is a great position to practice to relieve stiffness in your neck and shoulders. It opens the heart and also expands the ribcage allowing easier breathing.

- Lie down on your back, legs straight out and feet together.
- Place your palms under your thighs, palms facing down.

- Inhale slowly while pressing your elbows into the ground and arching your back and resting the top of your head on the floor.
- Exhale slowly and then breathe slowly while holding this position.

Chakra six: The Third eye chakra

This chakra focuses on our wisdom, insight, mind and intuition. When the following positions are practiced they can help heal many things such as vision, imagination and our ability to learn from different experiences. Physically it can help us with strokes, brain tumors and learning disabilities.

Position one: The Fish

This is the same position that was mentioned in the fifth chakras!

Position two: The tree

This position will help bring you inner peace, balance and strengthen your concentration levels; this position needs to be practices regularly to gain results:

- Stand up straight, wrap one leg around the other and press your hands together in the prayer pose in front of you.

- Balance yourself and then lift your hands above your head, palms still together.
- Focus your energy on the third eye and hold for as long as possible.

Chakras seven: The Crown Chakras

There are many issues which can be healed in the seventh chakras such as; intelligence, self knowledge, inspiration and depression. There are also many physical elements which can be healed from physical disorder to chronic exhaustion.

Position one: The Dog

This position is great for strengthening your balance!

- Kneel with your knees straight out under your hips and your hands on the floor in line with your shoulders.
- Inhaling slowly, lift your pelvic bone and keep your head down. Exhale slowly.
- Hold this position and breathe in and out slowly.
- Lower your body back to the kneeling position, place your forehead on the floor and relax for a couple minutes.

Position two: The Lotus

This is a classic yoga posture which works fantastic with Reiki healing.

- Sit down with your spine as straight as possible and your legs folded in front of you. Place your feet up onto your knees.
- This will bring strength to your core and holding this position will increase your powers of concentration for all Reiki healing.

All these yoga positions are great in their own ways at helping your heal the chakras, focus on the areas that your feel need healing and practice the positions regularly. Practicing the positions will enhance the effect that they have on you.

Enjoy and relax!

Chapter 11
Benefits of Reiki Healing (You Can't Miss This!)

Due to the fact that Reiki is a way of healing physically, emotionally, spiritually and mentally it can have many different benefits to many different aspects of life.

- **Deep Relaxation**: due to relaxed nature of Reiki healing, it can make you very relaxed and calm. This is a great way to unwind and release stress from your body.

- **Increase in personal energy**: as your body will be relaxed and healed it will also be re-energised and you may find yourself having more energy to do activities with your friends and families.

- **Balance of inner peace**: your body will feel healed and also re-energised therefore leading to your body having an inner peace and sense of happiness.

- **Pain Relief**: as Reiki healing is a way of releasing any pain that you may be feeling, you will have a sense of pain relief with continuous treatments.

- **Improved sleep pattern**: due to your body being completely relaxed and healed you may notice a change in your sleep patterns, you may sleep heavier and for longer periods of time.

- **Spiritual clarity**: as Reiki treatments are very spiritual you may experience some spiritual clarity.

- **Clears draining emotions**: Reiki should help clear any draining emotions that you may be experiencing from distress, grief and sorrow.

- **Improved blood circulation**: it can be a great treatment or cure for those suffering with bad blood circulation; it will help improve your blood circulation by relieving your body from unwanted stress and pain.

- **Helps treat symptoms of unbalance**: there are many symptoms of unbalance that can be treated through Reiki such as; stress related disorders, migraines, chronic fatigue, insomnia, depression, menopause, sinus related conditions and asthma.

- **Surgery recovery**: the treatment of Reiki has been seen to increase the speed of surgery recovery and decrease the intensity of side effects that may occur.

- **Purifying environments**: Reiki can be used to remove the negative energy from many work environments such as; offices, treatment rooms and homes.

- **Faster healing**: it has been shown that Reiki can help heal athlete's injuries quicker.

- **Supports the immune system**: with continuous treatment you may find that you have a stronger immune system and are not as likely to be affected by common illnesses such as colds.

- **Encourages self healing**: you may notice with on-going treatment that your body is able to deal with pain and illnesses a lot better than before.

Conclusion

Thank you so much for downloading this book and joining me on the journey of creating a healthier you! Did you get the family involved? Did you enjoy it?

I hope that the knowledge, tips and exercises shown in this book have helped you experience Reiki healing and have allowed you and your family to have fun at the same time. Have you developed your own exercises? Created your own Reiki healing techniques that work for you?

Share them with your friends and allow them to experience the healing powers of Reiki!
I hope that the information provided has been empowering and has given you a clear understanding of Reiki and what it can do to benefit your life. Once you have learnt the ability to use Reiki it will be with you for the rest of our life, it will promote a healthier lifestyle which I am sure all your friends and family members will notice.

Help your friends and family enjoy the same benefits as you, teach them how to experience the spiritual and personal growth, it can be a life-changing experience!

Most of all please enjoy your new healthier lifestyle. It will take practice and patience but you will see the benefits start to show the more your practice the basic techniques.

Once again thank you for downloading this book and taking the time to learn the healing benefits and ways to Reiki!

To your success!
Dominique Francon

Preview Of "Buddhism For Beginners! - The Ultimate Guide To Incorporate Buddhism Into Your Life – A Buddhism Approach For More Energy, Focus, And Inner Peace"

Introduction
Buddhism CAN Change Your Life, Did You Know That?

There's a common misconception that Buddhism is somehow *harder* than Christianity. Think about Christianity: it's easy, right? So, if someone alien were to ask you to describe Christianity, what would you say to them?

Would you describe the imagery of Catholicism, the relevance of the Virgin Mary and emphasis on confessions before God?

Would you talk about the evolution of Protestantism, starting with Martin Luther and how Christianity aims to guide people to be more like Jesus Christ in their actions?

Would you start even further back, all the way back to the writing of the Bible? Before or after the Old Testament? To be truly accurate you'd have to include Abraham and Isaac, and explain most of Judaism while you're at it.

Would you talk about Episcopalians? The United Church? The Westboro Baptist Church? Anglicans? Jehovah's Witnesses? Gospel choirs? The Crusades?

In other words: where do you start, and where do you end?

The fact is that all religions are extremely complex, and Buddhism is no different. Buddhism can't be boiled down into a single phrase: "It's about achieving a Zen understanding of the world, and feeling at peace"—that only begins to describe some of the complexities of a proper Buddhist lifestyle.

But that doesn't mean that Buddhism is difficult to learn. That's why I'm writing this book. I want to help you understand Buddhism from a ground-level, from a totally introductory standpoint, so you can take from it what you'd like. This book isn't meant to convert you to any religion (everyone knows that, as far as conversions go, Buddhists are probably the least likely), but it instead aims to guide you towards understanding what has been the dominant eastern religion for over 2,000 years.

Buddhism isn't alone in this respect—there's divergence with Hinduism, Taoism and Japanese Zen philosophy. They're roughly similar in the way that Judaism, Christianity and Islam are similar—

which they are, actually, because they're all based on the same original stories of Abraham and Isaac, and all deify a supremely powerful being, just in different forms. (The Jewish God was later split into three—the Father, the Son and the Holy Spirit—and Muslims interpreted Him as Allah—but He's actually the same guy in every instance.)

Similarly, there are a myriad forms of Buddhism: Mahayana, Theravada, Cheontae, Zen, Nichiren, Shingon… the list goes on.

And, in fact, Buddhism shares many moral and ethical similarities with Christianity and Judaism. Pretty much every religion, at the end of the day, advocates being a good person, doing good deeds, not committing crimes and helping others. In all respects, education and wisdom is revered over all. Buddhism is much the same. Consider this quote: "Drop by drop is the water pot filled. Likewise, the wise man, gathering it little by little, fills himself with good."

Literally any religious figure could have gotten away with saying that. But you know what? It was the original Buddha.

In order to get the most out of Buddhism and help your day-to-day life, we're not going to focus on the little differences between Buddhism sects. I'll introduce them to you in the first two chapters, along with what Buddhism teaches and what the religion is all about *in a nutshell*, because it's important to grasp the key concepts if you want to understand how to implement it in your life. Then we'll discuss what Buddhism teaches us on a practical level, dealing with subjects such as living in the present moment, the power of meditation and yoga (which are, actually, more similar than you might believe) and how the age-old concept of karma—including rebirth and how good deeds beget happiness—can help guide us through everyday life, even if we don't believe it literally.

The fact is, like all religions, it is not only difficult but extremely dangerous to follow it 100 percent. We've come to a point as a global society—with the ease of access to information that the internet has provided, and now that we can hear so many different viewpoints, philosophies and religious beliefs—that individualizing is becoming important and popular. There's a reason that every religion is seeing smaller and smaller numbers each year. Churches report lower attendance records, and most Jews identify more with the secular Woody Allen and Jerry Seinfeld than the ancient wise man Rabbi Hillel.

And more than that, we're learning that it's not a crime to dip into multiple religions. You can turn the other cheek like Jesus says, and also celebrate Passover with your Jewish friends. We've successfully convinced ourselves that, as long as we are true and decent people, which God we believe in matters less than how we live our lives.

And you know what? That's what Buddhism teaches us.

Buddhism is a *nontheistic* religion. That means Buddhists don't believe in a One Almighty God. Buddhists instead try to find inner peace, within themselves, not relying on an outside being to teach them. It is a religion based on self-importance, self-respect and, perhaps most importantly, self-discipline. That makes it easy to adopt certain Buddhist practices into our daily lives. Heck, we do it already, all the time—think of yoga, or mantras, or we repeat to ourselves, or the belief in good and bad karma, or meditation. These are all phrases and acts adopted from Buddhism, which have seeped into our everyday lives and our everyday vocabulary.

When you think of it that way, Buddhism isn't so foreign.

But wait, you might be saying. Back up a second. If there's no God, then who are all those statues of? Who's the big fat laughing guy, and the snarling big-eared one? And who was the original Buddha, if not a God?

And you know what? I'm going to answer all those questions in the upcoming chapters. There are too many questions. Questions are crucial in Buddhism—it's a good thing to ask them. Hopefully, I'll be able to answer as many as I can.

The fact is that Buddhism, as we know it today, has been around for over 2,000 years and has been the foundation of dozens of civilizations—some successful, some now extinct. Buddhist structures, statues and temples are some of the most historically enduring and spiritually meaningful monuments in the world: think of Cambodia's mighty Ankor Wat, a massive temple complex over 1,000-years-old; Borobudur, a magnificent ancient stone pyramid in central Java, Indonesia, that welcome a gorgeous sunrise every morning; the Hill Temple, nestled between vibrant green trees and overlooking the ancient city of Kyoto, Japan; Thailand's Wat Pho, with a famously luxurious-looking reclining Buddha, said to be the birthplace of Thai massage; and South Korea's colorful temples, like Guinsa and Haeinsa, filled with chanting monks and towering stone pagodas.

Buddhism is no joke. It's not a small belief, and it's historically older than our Biblical realities, dating back to the 5th and 6th century BC. There's no excuse to be ignorant of what the eastern half of the world believes, and there's no reason we can't learn from it.

So, for now, put your mind at ease. Put on some soft, meditative music. And let's get started.

Chapter 1
Who the First Buddha Was & What He Taught

There once was a man, around 2,600 years ago, who was born in northern India, in the foothills of the Himalayan mountains, which is now part of southern Nepal. His name was Siddhartha Gautama. Gautama was born into royalty as an opulent young aristocratic prince, with a life surrounded by comfort and luxury.

But Gautama had a problem: he wasn't very happy. It's the age-old story of "money can't buy you happiness," and it doesn't buy Gautama any joy at all. He finds himself confused, restless and constantly questioning of everything. He had a philosophical mind.

So, discouraged by his lifestyle, Gautama left his palace at the age of 29 in search of greater meaning in the world. This was the first time he had left home and witnessed the outside world. He saw the problems of the world for the first time: the sick, the old, the suffering. The naïve prince was eager to learn more about these real-world problems. He started going on more trips outside the palace to interact with people more people who were diseased, vain and dying. These problems depressed him immensely, and he decided to change his lifestyle completely.

He became an ascetic—one who abstains from mortal pleasures. He threw himself into a world devoid of expensive belongings and material wealth, and began begging for alms, pure charity, in the street. His goal was humility.

Eventually someone spotted and recognized him (as a prince, you'd think it wouldn't take too long) and tried to bring him back to the world of royalty. He denied this offer, too, and instead changed course: he began seeking out every great philosophical mind of his time, looking for answers to his problems of happiness.

He went to practice yogic meditation with the masters, and excelled at it to the point of being offered to succeed the masters as a permanent teacher, but Gautama denied this offer, too. He tried a different sort of yoga under a different teacher, and attained a high plateau of meditative consciousness—again, impressed with his determination, the then-master asked him to stay. But Gautama still wasn't satisfied.

He then turned to self-mortification: a deeper kind of humility. He deprived himself of all worldly luxuries, including food. Allegedly eating only a single leaf or nut per day, he nearly starved himself to death. He wanted no part of any world that would continue to offer him luxuries of any sort, including status as a "master" or "king". The very thought of hierarchy put a bad taste in his mouth.

By now he was 35-years-old, and found himself sitting beneath what has today become famous as the Bodhi Tree, now in Bodh Gaya, India, in the distant groves near the Neranjara riverbanks. He fell, nearly unconscious due to starvation, and promised himself he wouldn't wake up until he'd found enlightenment. He then fell into a deep meditative state, and found a previously unimaginable state of clear and thorough consciousness. He began thinking about the world, the universe, the nature of life.

This took 49 days, so the legend goes.

From that point on, he was known as the Buddha—or, later, once more Buddhas start popping up throughout history (and yes, there are at least 28 more; but no, we won't get into all of them in as much detail), he became known as the Supreme Buddha. "Buddha" means, simply, "Awakened One" or "Enlightened One," so the title fits.

What Did He Learn?

It's complicated, even impossible, to know exactly what he thought that night he underwent enlightenment. Certainly, at the very least, he shoved aside asceticism and self-mortification, along with self-indulgence at every level. He essentially created Buddhism as we know it today, and though what exactly that means can be vague, he does provide some helpful guides, which are known as dharma.

He wrote down his newfound doctrine based on what we know as "The Four Noble Truths", through which followers of Buddhism can reach Nirvana. Nirvana is the end goal in Buddhism: it is a state of awesome freedom, total ease of mind and mental mastery. To translate it into religious terms, it's heaven on earth. Anyone can reach a state of mental nirvana through dedication to Buddhism and following the teachings of Gautama.

To be in a state of nirvana means to ignore greed, selfishness, anger and other distracting emotions. It is, in a word, to be emotionally *above* the rest of the world. It sounds a bit haughty, but the idea is this completely carelessness about oneself, a delicate balance between being self-centered and not being egocentric. Nirvana means being altruistic and kind, understanding selflessness enough to know how small you are in the universe, and being okay with that.

According to one story, immediately after waking up from his Enlightenment, the Buddha wasn't sure if he should teach others his dharma. He wasn't sure everyone could handle it: after all, humans are afflicted by greed and ignorance all the time, which is why he had to go through this six-year meditative process to figure it out at all. Buddha told his problem to a friend, who convinced him that at least some people will grasp his meaning. Buddha agreed to have faith, and so the dharma was born into public.

What Does He Teach?

We're going to break down Buddhism really simply for you now, just because, well, this is an eBook, and we have a lot of other topics to touch on. So excuse me as I skip some of the details and sections like the Five Skandhas and Six Realms, which basically explain how to view life, and instead focus on what the Supreme Buddha wants *you* to learn.

The Four Noble Truths

There are four realities to face when you look at the world. The Four Noble Truths were what the Supreme Buddha first taught in his very first sermons to the public, so this is very Buddha-101 appropriate.

The first truth is that *there is suffering in the world*. We may know this phrase as, "Shit happens." Basically, life can be difficult—loved ones get hit by cars, our pets get cancer, we get fired, babies die in the womb, an African child just died as you read this sentence, schools get shot up; even if you avoid all of this, in the best-case scenario, you're going to die one day. Basically, there is pain, strife and difficulty. This is a truth of the world, and the first one we must face in order to achieve enlightenment: even if our own particular lives are mostly okay (i.e. none of the above apply, save for the death bit), the world is a harsh and brutal place. The First Noble Truth tells us that we must mentally face this head-on: think about it. Believe in it. Confront it.

The second truth defines this suffering: *every suffering has a cause*. There are a few causes. One is a craving for something: for respect, for power, for control, for material happiness. The other reasons we suffer are because we are trying to define ourselves as something we are not, or do not want to be; for example, if we're sad but want to be happy, we are trying to redefine ourselves in that moment. We try to unite with experiences in the way that we want to be constantly connected to the outside world, have a past, present and future life, and be successful. Or else we crave the opposite: to not feel sad when we don't want to, or to escape from painful emotions.

The Third Noble Truth is that *your suffering can end*. It is possible, in other words, to remove ourselves from our problems. We can rethink our lives, and redefine our personalities. Once we realize how loosely tied we are to our personalities, we can work on new ones. We don't need to pretend to fit in when we don't. We don't need to impress people we don't get alone with. We could be simpler than that, and focus on affirming ourselves to ourselves alone. We need to remove the cravings from the Second Noble Truth and focus on our real needs.

The fourth and final Noble Truth is *how to end the suffering*. It's a subtle wording difference from number three, but a significant one: while three tells us *that we can* end our suffering, four begins to tell us *how*. The answer is, basically, mindful meditation; in a longer answer, the path to happiness involves what's called **The Eightfold Path**.

The Eightfold Path

The Eightfold Path is crucial to every Buddhist practice, and comprises the Fourth Noble Truth in its entirety. It is the path to enlightenment, true understanding and personal happiness.

At the risk of turning this chapter into an extremely dense introduction, I'm going to go over the Eightfold Path very quickly, in point-form, so as to not overload you all at once.

The Noble Eightfold Path is divided into eight ways to act correctly. They're called the Rights. So remember that when you read Right here, it means Right as in Objectively Correct.

The eight Rights are divided into three sub-sections, including Wisdom, Ethical Conduct and Concentration.

The two filed under *Wisdom* describe a proper Buddhist mental state:

1. **Right View** – Sometimes called "Right Perspective" or "Right Outlook", this can be summed up as the proper way of looking at the nature of things, the way the world exists in its natural form, which can adopt an almost scientific perspective: physics, chemistry and biology all dictate our world.

2. **Right Thought** – Thinking good thoughts will give you a good life. To achieve this you must mentally renounce material goods and think instead about what matters: good deeds, peacekeeping, charity and being kind towards others.

The three steps under *Ethical Conduct* progress this lifestyle into reality:

3. **Right Speech** – So, you've got those good thoughts in your head? Speak them. No lying, no wasteful chitchat, no insults.

4. **Right Action** – Talk is cheap—do good deeds. Don't kill, steal or rape.

5. **Right Livelihood** – Don't make your job an evil one. Don't create weapons, don't trade slaves, don't sell drugs, don't kill people. According to Buddha, the "business of meat" is also a no-no; sorry, butchers.

The last three, under *Concentration*, might be the hardest to achieve:

6. **Right Effort** – This describes preventative measures. If you're leading a true Buddhist life, you will need effort to actively subdue your material and worldly urges. Be mindful of the good that has no yet risen within yourself, and abstain from the evil.

7. **Right Mindfulness** – Also translated as "Right Memory", to be mindful of something means you're keeping it in mind. You should be constantly aware of every

part of your body, in tune with your health and mental state, to continue your other Right ways.

8. **Right Concentration** – Also known as "Right Meditation", this simply defines an ideal meditative state: one aloof from the world, purely tranquil and absorbed by your mental cleanness.

Phew! That about sums it up. Thanks for hanging in there. I know this stuff can get a little dense at times, but, as the Noble Eightfold Path shows, it's actually pretty natural. It's the same basic morality as suggested by Abrahamic religions: think good thoughts, do good deeds, and stay that way.

The big departures in Buddhism come in the specific logic of the religion. The description of the mind and body is different from the Christian conception of the soul. Nirvana is different from heaven. But only in logical terms.

If looked at abstractly, from a bit far away, you'll find that the first of the Four Noble Truths—that there is suffering in the world—is an issue debated and tackled by every major religion in the world. Others might simply chalk it up to the old phrase, "God works in mysterious ways." The big change in Buddhism is that it tries to define that problem and, instead of promoting belief in God or Jesus to save you from such dangers and bring you to heaven, the Supreme Buddha suggests believing in yourself and overcoming these worldly problems while you're still on Earth.

This is by no means a comprehensive analysis—we still haven't gotten to karma, rebirth or the thousands of other little details that create Buddhism. But we'll get there soon.

For now, and in the next chapter, we're going to look at a few variations of Buddhism, and how it's affected the world as we know it.

To check out the rest of "Buddhism For Beginners! - The Ultimate Guide To Incorporate Buddhism Into Your Life – A Buddhism Approach For More Energy, Focus, And Inner Peace", **go to Amazon and look for it right now!**

Ps: You'll find many more books like these under my name, Dominique Francon.

Don't miss them! Here's a short list:

- Buddhism For Beginners
- Meditation For Beginners
- Reiki For Beginners
- Yoga For Beginners

- Running Will Make You FIT
- Cycling HIIT Training

- Paleo Recipe Cookbooks
- Much, much more!

About the Author

Dominique Francon is a significant health connoisseur devoted to helping others get healthy all around the world.

From a very young age, Francon understood the value and potential of leading a healthy lifestyle. And because of her genuine appreciation and enthusiasm for all things health-related, she has dedicated a great deal of time and effort to researching the best of what fitness, nutritional diets and overall wellbeing programs have to offer.

In the beginning, Francon focused on working with people in various gym and sports club settings. Before long she became exceedingly in tune with the health and fitness solutions that had the best results for her clients' issues and goals. But after years of accumulating one health expertise following another, Francon decided she wanted to reach out to even more individuals.

She wanted to help people on a bigger scale. For this reason she resolved to share her extensive knowledge with people through writing and publishing books pertaining to her vast health-related know-how. Currently she has authored books on such cutting-edge topics as paleo cooking, Zen, Yoga, running and cycling.

Francon has a real passion for all the subjects she writes about and she takes the job seriously. She knows self-development is, for a lot of people, as significant as it is for her. But she also knows how tough it is to change one's lifestyle. With this in mind, her aim while writing is to make the concepts and instructions as helpful and accessible to her readers as possible. After all, for her the end objective is improving the lives of others.